# The 'ug' Bug
## VI

By Viola & Zaida Stefano

**VeeZee Publications**

Copyright © VeeZee Publications Pty. Ltd. 2025

First published in Australia in 2025
by VeeZee Publications Pty. Ltd.

veezeepublications.com

The right of Viola Stefano to be identified as the author of this work have been asserted by her in accordance with the **Copyright Amendment (Moral Rights) Act 2000.**

All rights reserved. Apart from any use as permitted by the author & under the **Copyright Act 1968**, no part may be reproduced, copied, scanned, stored in a retrieval system, recorded, or shared, by any means or in any form, without prior written & signed authorization from the publisher.

ISBN: 978-1-923120-19-8

A catalogue record of this book is available from the **National Library of Australia.**

Author: Viola Stefano
Illustrations, cover & internal designs: Zaida Stefano

Illustrations copyright © Zaida Stefano 2025
Design copyright © Zaida Stefano 2025

**Disclaimer:** The content presented in this book is meant for educational purposes only. The author & publisher claim no accountability to any entity or person for any liability, damage, or loss caused or assumed to be caused directly or indirectly as a consequence of the application, use, or interpretation of the material in this book.

# Core words used in this book

| I | want | can | stop | look |
|---|---|---|---|---|
| like | more | he | go | see |
| here | what | do | the | and |
| out | where | we | it | up |
| not | they | when | that | down |
| she | now | them | is | put |
| help | off | you | yes | on |
| turn | who | this | no | why |
| done | make | a | to | under |
| come | in | some | which | there |
| open | get | good | same | home |

A pug sat on a rug.

The pug can see a bug.

The bug can see the pug.

The bug wants to

hug the pug.

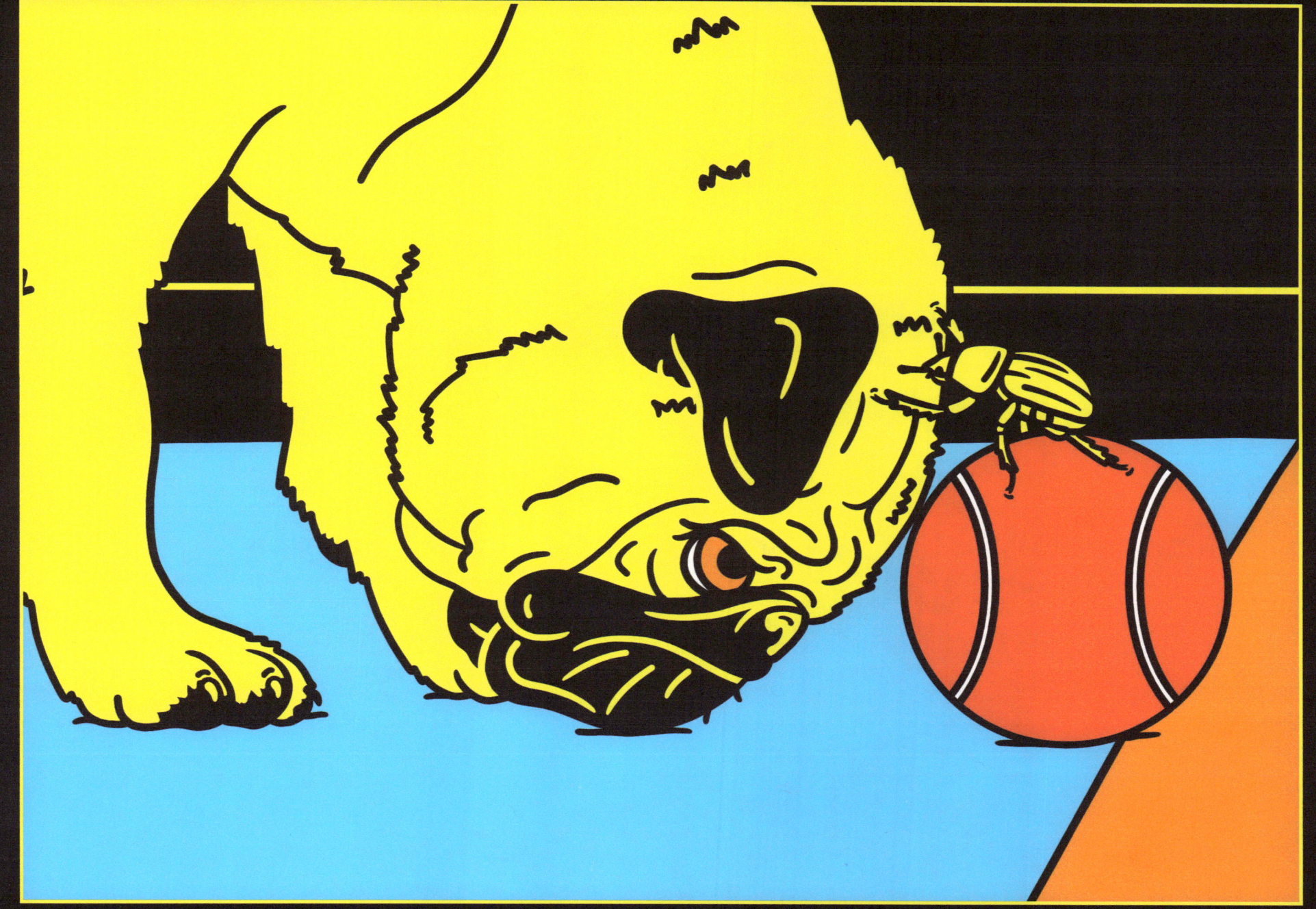

No! The pug does not want to hug the bug.

The bug crept under the rug.

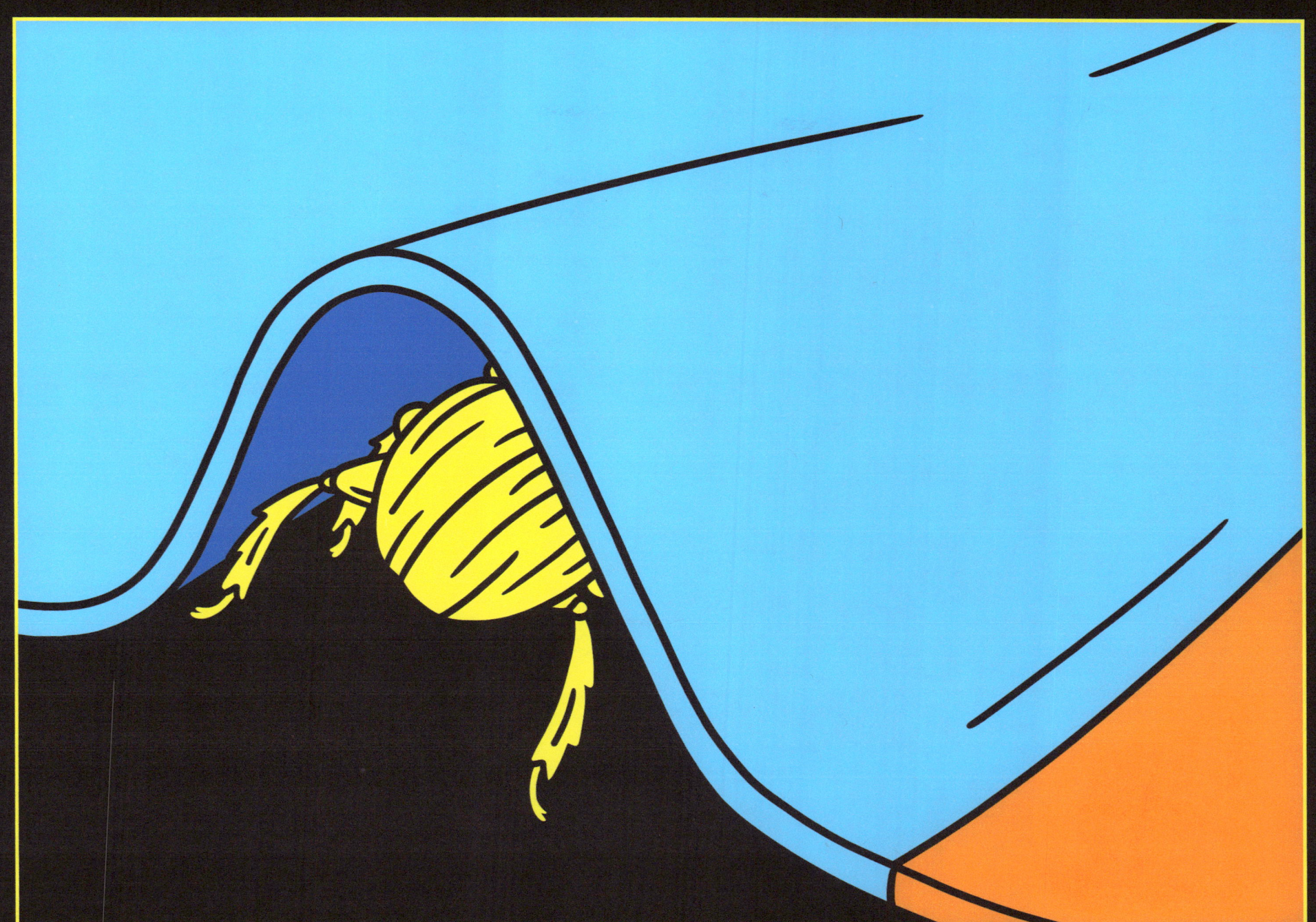

The pug sat on that rug.

The bug crept into the mug.

The pug sat near the mug.

"I want a hug", said the bug.

"Yes!" said the pug.

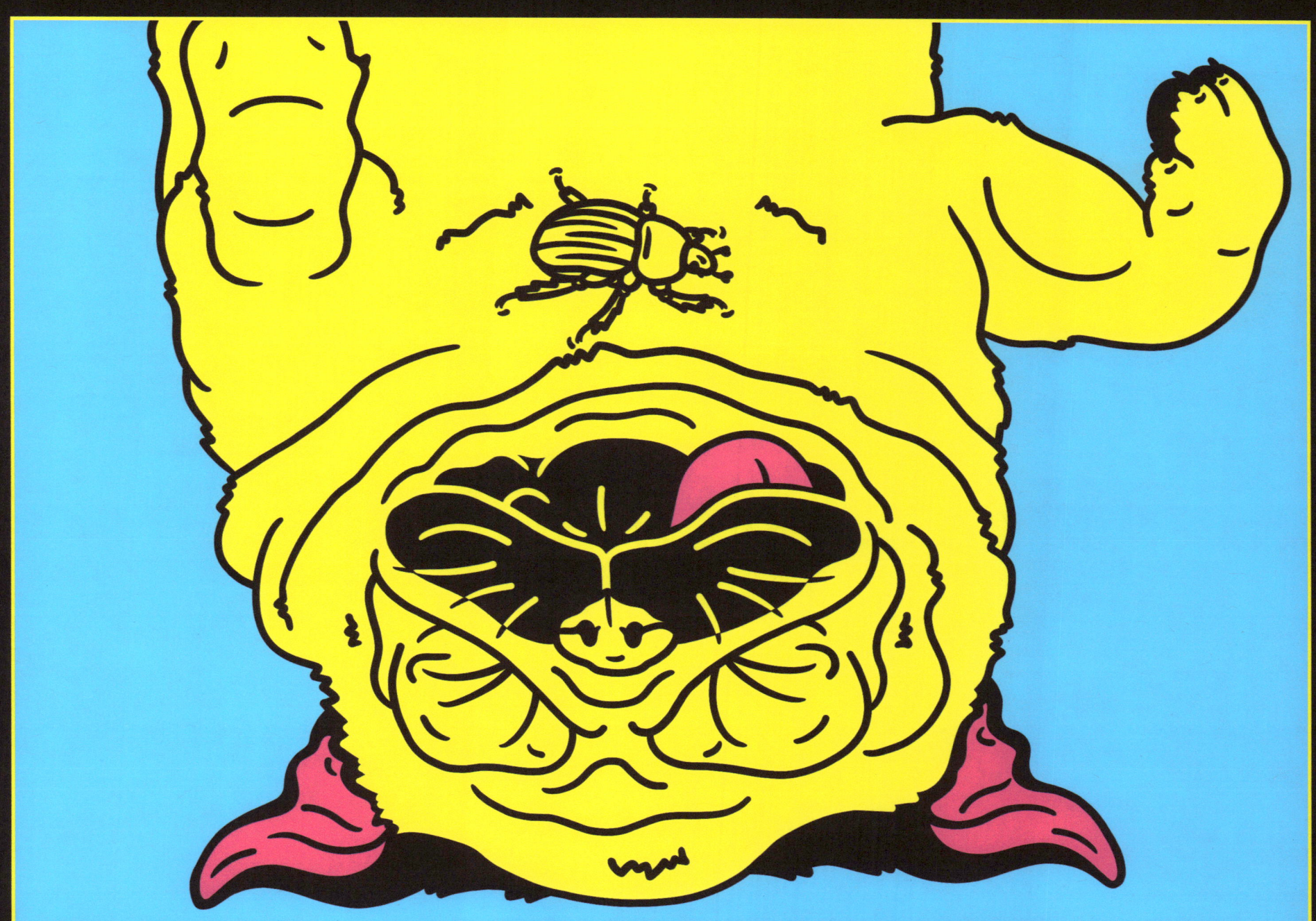

## Words that end in 'ug' in this book

| pug | rug | mug |
|-----|-----|-----|
| hug | bug |     |

## Words with 'u' in this book

| under |
|-------|

We hope you had fun reading!

# Learning made easy with VeeZee

**VeeZee Publications**

## Wait, there's more!

Visit our website for information about our range of readers & supporting products.

veezeepublications.com